Thank you to those that I have had the privilege to work with, manage and mentor.

It has been a pleasure.

Table Of Contents

Chapter 1: Understanding Different Management Styles — 4
- Introduction to Management Styles — 4
- Autocratic Management Style — 5
- Democratic Management Style — 6
- Laissez-faire Management Style — 7
- Transformational Leadership Style — 8
- Servant Leadership Style — 9
- Situational Leadership Style — 10
- Transactional Leadership Style — 11
- Charismatic Leadership Style — 12
- Bureaucratic Management Style — 13
- Adaptive Leadership Style — 14

Chapter 2: Embracing Servant Leadership as a New Manager — 15
- What is Servant Leadership? — 15
- Characteristics of a Servant Leader — 16
- Benefits of Servant Leadership — 17
- Challenges of Implementing Servant Leadership — 18
- Developing a Servant Heart — 19
- Leading by Example — 20
- Building Trust and Empathy — 21
- Fostering a Collaborative Environment — 23

    Encouraging Growth and Development   24

    Empowering Others   25

Chapter 3: Applying Situational Leadership in Real-world Scenarios   26

    Understanding Situational Leadership Theory   26

    Assessing Employee Readiness   27

    Adapting Your Leadership Style   28

    Providing Support and Guidance   29

    Delegating Responsibilities   30

    Communicating Effectively   31

    Handling Conflict and Challenges   33

    Evaluating Performance   34

    Continuous Improvement and Adaptation   35

Chapter 4: Integrating Adaptive Leadership Into Your Management Approach   36

    The Concept of Adaptive Leadership   36

    Embracing Change and Uncertainty   37

    Navigating Complex Situations   38

    Building Resilience and Flexibility   39

    Encouraging Innovation and Creativity   40

    Leading Through Crisis   41

    Engaging Stakeholders   42

    Embracing Diversity and Inclusion   43

    Enhancing Organizational Agility   44

    Sustaining Long-term Success   45

Chapter 5: Becoming a Well-rounded Leader in the Modern Workplace — 46

- Balancing Different Leadership Styles — 47
- Developing Your Personal Leadership Philosophy — 47
- Seeking Feedback and Continuous Learning — 48
- Building a Support Network — 49
- Leading with Integrity and Authenticity — 51
- Inspiring and Motivating Others — 52
- Cultivating a Positive Work Culture — 53
- Embracing the Journey of Leadership Growth — 54
- Making a Lasting Impact as a Servant Leader — 55
- Conclusion: Your Journey to Leading with a Servant Heart — 56

Chapter 1: Understanding Different Management Styles

Introduction to Management Styles

As a new manager, understanding different management styles is crucial to effectively lead your team and achieve organizational goals. Management styles refer to the way in which a manager interacts with their team, makes decisions, and guides the overall direction of the organization. Each management style has its own unique characteristics and can be effective in different situations. In this subchapter, we will explore various management styles, including autocratic, democratic, laissez-faire, transformational, servant, situational, transactional, charismatic, bureaucratic, and adaptive leadership styles.

Autocratic management style is characterized by a top-down approach where the manager makes all decisions without input from their team. While this style can be efficient in certain situations, it can also lead to disengagement and resentment among team members. On the other hand, democratic management style involves collaboration and input from team members in decision-making processes. This style fosters a sense of ownership and empowerment among employees, leading to higher levels of engagement and productivity.

Laissez-faire management style is hands-off and allows team members to have a high degree of autonomy in their work. While this style can be effective with self-motivated and skilled employees, it may lead to confusion and lack of direction in some cases. Transformational leadership style focuses on inspiring and motivating team members to achieve a common goal. Servant leadership style emphasizes serving the needs of others before one's own, fostering a culture of empathy, trust, and collaboration within the team.

Situational leadership style recognizes that different situations require different approaches to leadership. This style involves adapting your leadership style to the needs of your team and the specific circumstances at hand. Transactional leadership style is based on a system of rewards and punishments to motivate team members to achieve goals. Charismatic leadership style involves inspiring and motivating others through charisma and personality. Bureaucratic management style relies on rules and procedures to guide decision-making and ensure consistency within the organization. Adaptive leadership style involves being flexible and innovative in response to changing circumstances and challenges. Each of these management styles has its own strengths and weaknesses, and as a new manager, it is important to understand when and how to apply each style effectively in different situations.

Autocratic Management Style

In the world of management, there are various styles that leaders can adopt to guide their teams towards success. One such style is the autocratic management style, which is characterized by a top-down approach where the leader makes decisions without input from their team members. This type of leadership is often associated with a strict hierarchy and a focus on results rather than relationships.

New managers who adopt an autocratic management style may find that their team members feel disempowered and demotivated. This can lead to a lack of creativity and innovation within the team, as team members may feel hesitant to speak up or share their ideas. Additionally, this style of management can create a sense of fear and resentment among team members, leading to a toxic work environment.

Despite these drawbacks, there are situations where an autocratic management style may be necessary. For example, in times of crisis or when quick decisions need to be made, a leader may need to take charge and make decisions without consulting their team. However, it is important for new managers to recognize when to use this style and when to adopt a more collaborative approach.

As new managers grow and develop in their role, they may find that a more democratic or servant leadership style is more effective in motivating and empowering their team members. These styles focus on building strong relationships, fostering open communication, and empowering team members to take ownership of their work. By embracing these styles, new managers can create a positive work environment where team members feel valued and supported.

In conclusion, while the autocratic management style may have its time and place, new managers should strive to adopt more collaborative and empowering leadership styles in order to build strong, successful teams. By leading with a servant heart and focusing on the growth and development of their team members, new managers can create a positive and productive work environment that fosters creativity, innovation, and success.

Democratic Management Style

In the realm of management styles, the democratic management style stands out as a popular and effective approach that empowers employees and fosters collaboration within the workplace. As a new manager, understanding and implementing this style can lead to a more engaged and motivated team.

One of the key principles of the democratic management style is involving employees in the decision-making process. By seeking input and feedback from team members, a manager can tap into the collective knowledge and expertise of the group, leading to better decisions and increased buy-in from employees. This collaborative approach also helps to build trust and mutual respect between managers and their team members.

In contrast to the autocratic management style, where decisions are made unilaterally by the manager, the democratic management style values the input and opinions of all team members. This inclusive approach not only leads to better decision-making but also creates a more positive and supportive work environment where employees feel valued and respected.

Another benefit of the democratic management style is its ability to promote innovation and creativity within the team. By encouraging open communication and brainstorming sessions, managers can tap into the diverse perspectives and ideas of their team members, leading to new and innovative solutions to challenges and opportunities.

Overall, the democratic management style is a powerful tool for new managers looking to build strong, cohesive teams and drive positive results. By embracing this approach and valuing the input and contributions of all team members, managers can create a culture of trust, collaboration, and mutual respect that fosters growth and success for both individuals and the organization as a whole.

Laissez-faire Management Style

As a new manager, it is important to understand the various management styles that exist in the business world. One such style is the laissez-faire management style, which translates to "hands-off" in French. This approach involves giving employees the freedom to work without constant supervision or micromanagement.

Laissez-faire management style is often seen as a more laid-back approach to leadership, where employees are encouraged to take ownership of their work and make decisions independently. This style can be beneficial in certain situations, particularly when working with highly skilled and self-motivated employees who thrive in a more autonomous work environment.

However, it is important to note that the laissez-faire management style is not suitable for all situations or all employees. Some individuals may require more guidance and direction from their managers in order to succeed. It is crucial for new managers to assess the needs and abilities of their team members before deciding to adopt a laissez-faire approach.

One of the key benefits of the laissez-faire management style is that it can foster creativity and innovation among employees. By allowing individuals the freedom to work in their own way, new ideas and approaches can emerge that may not have been possible in a more rigidly structured environment.

Overall, the laissez-faire management style can be a valuable tool in a manager's leadership toolbox, but it should be used judiciously and in the right circumstances. By understanding the strengths and limitations of this approach, new managers can effectively navigate the complexities of leading a diverse team and cultivate a productive work environment for all.

Transformational Leadership Style

Transformational leadership is a management style that focuses on inspiring and motivating employees to achieve their full potential. This leadership style is characterized by a leader who is charismatic, visionary, and able to communicate a compelling vision for the organization. Transformational leaders are able to inspire their teams to go above and beyond what is expected of them, and to work towards a shared vision of success.

One of the key characteristics of transformational leadership is the ability to build strong relationships with employees. Transformational leaders are able to connect with their team members on a personal level, and to build trust and rapport with them. By developing strong relationships with employees, transformational leaders are able to create a positive and supportive work environment, where employees feel valued and motivated to perform at their best.

Another important aspect of transformational leadership is the ability to inspire and motivate employees. Transformational leaders are able to communicate a compelling vision for the organization, and to inspire their teams to work towards that vision. By setting high standards for performance and providing support and encouragement to employees, transformational leaders are able to motivate their teams to achieve their full potential.

In addition to inspiring and motivating employees, transformational leaders are also able to empower their teams to take ownership of their work. Transformational leaders delegate responsibility to their team members, and trust them to make decisions and take initiative. By empowering employees to take ownership of their work, transformational leaders are able to create a culture of accountability and responsibility within the organization.

Overall, transformational leadership is a powerful management style that can help new managers to inspire and motivate their teams to achieve great results. By focusing on building strong relationships, inspiring and motivating employees, and empowering them to take ownership of their work, transformational leaders can create a positive and productive work environment where employees are motivated to perform at their best.

Servant Leadership Style

In the world of management styles, one that is gaining popularity and recognition is the Servant Leadership style. This approach focuses on serving the needs of others before considering one's own interests, making it a unique and powerful way to lead a team. As new managers, embracing the Servant Leadership style can lead to positive outcomes for both the team and the organization as a whole.

One key aspect of the Servant Leadership style is putting the needs of your team members first. This means actively listening to their concerns, providing support and guidance, and empowering them to succeed in their roles. By fostering a culture of trust and collaboration, new managers can create a positive work environment where team members feel valued and motivated to perform at their best.

Another important characteristic of Servant Leadership is leading by example. As a new manager, it is essential to demonstrate the values and behaviors you expect from your team members. By showing humility, empathy, and a strong commitment to serving others, you can inspire your team to follow your lead and work towards common goals.

Servant Leadership also emphasizes the importance of building strong relationships with team members. By taking the time to get to know your employees on a personal level, you can better understand their strengths, weaknesses, and motivations. This knowledge allows you to tailor your leadership approach to each individual, providing the support and guidance they need to succeed.

In conclusion, the Servant Leadership style offers new managers a unique and effective approach to leading a team. By focusing on serving the needs of others, leading by example, and building strong relationships, new managers can create a positive work environment where team members feel valued, motivated, and empowered to succeed. Embracing this style of leadership can lead to long-term success for both the team and the organization as a whole.

Situational Leadership Style

In the world of leadership, there are many different styles that managers can adopt to lead their teams effectively. One popular approach is the Situational Leadership Style, which emphasizes the need for leaders to adapt their leadership style to fit the current situation and the needs of their team members. This approach recognizes that effective leadership is not a "one size fits all" proposition, and that leaders must be flexible and responsive to the ever-changing dynamics of the workplace.

The Situational Leadership Style is based on the idea that there is no single best way to lead a team, and that the most effective leaders are those who can adjust their approach to meet the unique needs of their team members. This means that leaders must be able to assess the current situation, evaluate the skills and abilities of their team members, and then choose the most appropriate leadership style to help their team achieve its goals.

One of the key principles of the Situational Leadership Style is the concept of "readiness," which refers to the ability and willingness of team members to take on new tasks and responsibilities. Leaders must assess the readiness of their team members and then adjust their leadership style accordingly. For example, if a team member is new to a task and lacks the necessary skills and experience, a more directive leadership approach may be needed. On the other hand, if a team member is highly skilled and motivated, a more hands-off, delegative approach may be more appropriate.

The Situational Leadership Style also emphasizes the importance of communication and feedback. Leaders must be able to provide clear direction and guidance to their team members, while also being open to feedback and input from their team. By fostering open communication and a culture of trust, leaders can ensure that their team members feel supported and empowered to take on new challenges and responsibilities.

In conclusion, the Situational Leadership Style is a valuable tool for new managers looking to develop their leadership skills. By recognizing the importance of adapting their approach to fit the current situation and the needs of their team members, leaders can create a more dynamic and effective work environment. By focusing on readiness, communication, and feedback, leaders can build strong, high-performing teams that are capable of achieving their goals and objectives.

Transactional Leadership Style

Transactional leadership style is a widely recognized approach to management that focuses on the exchange of rewards and punishments to motivate employees. This leadership style is characterized by clear expectations, structured guidelines, and a focus on achieving specific goals and objectives. In a transactional leadership model, managers reward employees for meeting performance targets and enforce consequences for failing to meet expectations. This approach is often seen as a more traditional and directive style of leadership, where the leader plays a central role in decision-making and goal-setting.

One of the key principles of transactional leadership is the idea of the "transaction" between the leader and their followers. This transaction involves a clear exchange of rewards and punishments based on performance and compliance with organizational policies and procedures. By setting up these clear expectations and consequences, transactional leaders are able to create a structured and predictable work environment that can help drive employee motivation and performance.

Transactional leaders also tend to be more task-oriented and focused on achieving specific outcomes. They are often hands-on in their approach to management, closely monitoring employee performance and providing feedback on a regular basis. This can help ensure that employees are meeting their targets and staying on track to achieve organizational goals.

While transactional leadership can be effective in certain situations, it is not without its drawbacks. Some critics argue that this style of leadership can lead to a lack of creativity and innovation among employees, as they may feel constrained by the rigid guidelines and expectations set by their managers. Additionally, the focus on rewards and punishments can sometimes create a culture of compliance rather than true engagement and commitment from employees.

Overall, transactional leadership can be a useful tool for new managers looking to establish clear expectations and drive performance within their teams. By understanding the principles of transactional leadership and how to effectively implement them, managers can create a structured and goal-oriented work environment that can help drive success for their organization.

Charismatic Leadership Style

In the world of leadership, there are many different styles that can be utilized to guide a team to success. One of the most well-known styles is the charismatic leadership style. Charismatic leaders are often seen as charming, inspiring, and confident individuals who have the ability to motivate and influence others through their strong personality and vision.

Charismatic leaders have a magnetic presence that draws others to them. They are often able to inspire their team members to achieve great things by sharing their passion and enthusiasm for a common goal. These leaders are able to create a sense of excitement and energy that can be infectious, motivating others to work towards a shared vision.

One of the key traits of a charismatic leader is their ability to communicate effectively. They are often skilled orators who can capture the attention of their audience and inspire them to take action. Charismatic leaders are able to articulate their vision in a way that resonates with others, making it easy for team members to understand and get on board with their goals.

Another important aspect of the charismatic leadership style is the ability to build strong relationships with team members. Charismatic leaders are often seen as approachable and empathetic, making it easy for others to trust and follow them. By fostering a sense of camaraderie and teamwork, these leaders are able to create a positive and supportive work environment where everyone feels valued and motivated to succeed.

Overall, the charismatic leadership style can be a powerful tool for new managers looking to inspire and motivate their team members. By embodying the traits of a charismatic leader, managers can cultivate a sense of passion, enthusiasm, and unity within their team, leading to increased productivity and success. By mastering the art of charismatic leadership, new managers can set themselves apart and become truly influential leaders in their organizations.

Bureaucratic Management Style

In the world of management styles, one that is often misunderstood and sometimes even maligned is the bureaucratic management style. This style is characterized by a strict adherence to rules, regulations, and procedures, with decision-making centralized at the top of the organizational hierarchy. While some may view this style as inflexible and stifling, there are actually some benefits to be found in its approach.

One of the key strengths of the bureaucratic management style is its emphasis on consistency and predictability. By clearly outlining roles, responsibilities, and procedures, employees know exactly what is expected of them and can work efficiently within the established framework. This can lead to increased productivity and a sense of stability within the organization.

However, one of the potential drawbacks of the bureaucratic management style is its tendency to stifle creativity and innovation. Because decisions are made at the top and must be adhered to without question, there is less room for experimentation and risk-taking. This can lead to a lack of adaptability in the face of changing circumstances, which can be a significant disadvantage in today's fast-paced business environment.

As a new manager, it is important to understand the nuances of the bureaucratic management style and how it can be effectively applied in certain situations. While it may not be the most popular or trendy management style, there are times when its focus on hierarchy and structure can be beneficial. By learning how to balance the rigidity of bureaucracy with the need for flexibility and innovation, you can become a more well-rounded and effective leader.

Ultimately, the key to success as a manager lies in understanding the strengths and weaknesses of all the different management styles and knowing when to adapt your approach to best suit the needs of your team and organization. By familiarizing yourself with the various styles, including the bureaucratic management style, you can develop the skills and knowledge necessary to lead with confidence and effectiveness in any situation.

Adaptive Leadership Style

Adaptive leadership style is a crucial aspect of effective management that new managers must understand and implement in their leadership approach. This style of leadership involves being flexible and responsive to the needs and challenges of the team and the organization as a whole. It requires the leader to adapt their leadership style based on the specific situation they are facing, rather than relying on a one-size-fits-all approach.

One of the key principles of adaptive leadership is the ability to assess and understand the current situation and make adjustments as needed. This may involve changing communication strategies, decision-making processes, or team dynamics to better address the challenges at hand. By being adaptable, leaders can better navigate complex and ever-changing work environments, ensuring that their team remains productive and motivated.

In contrast to more rigid management styles like autocratic or bureaucratic leadership, adaptive leadership allows for greater creativity and innovation within the team. By encouraging team members to think outside the box and experiment with new ideas, adaptive leaders can foster a culture of continuous improvement and growth. This can lead to increased employee engagement and satisfaction, as team members feel empowered to contribute their unique skills and perspectives to the organization.

Adaptive leadership is particularly valuable in times of change or uncertainty, as it enables leaders to pivot quickly and effectively in response to new challenges. By remaining agile and open-minded, new managers can better navigate unexpected obstacles and seize opportunities for growth and development. This style of leadership also promotes a culture of learning and adaptation, where team members are encouraged to embrace change and take ownership of their own professional development.

Adaptive leadership is a powerful tool for new managers looking to succeed in today's fast-paced and dynamic work environment. By being flexible, responsive, and open to new ideas, leaders can inspire their teams to achieve greater levels of success and innovation. By incorporating adaptive leadership principles into their management style, new managers can build stronger, more resilient teams and drive positive change within their organizations.

Chapter 2: Embracing Servant Leadership as a New Manager

What is Servant Leadership?

Servant leadership is a management style that focuses on serving the needs of others before one's own. It is about putting the team first and prioritizing their growth and success. This approach is in stark contrast to more traditional management styles, such as autocratic or bureaucratic, which prioritize the leader's authority and control over the team.

In servant leadership, the manager acts as a servant to their team, supporting and empowering them to achieve their goals. This style emphasizes collaboration, empathy, and a deep understanding of the team members' needs and motivations. By putting the team first, servant leaders create a positive and inclusive work environment where everyone feels valued and supported.

One of the key principles of servant leadership is leading by example. A servant leader sets a high standard for themselves and expects the same from their team. They are willing to roll up their sleeves and work alongside their team members, showing that they are not above any task. This humility and willingness to serve inspire trust and respect among the team.

Servant leadership is also about developing the potential of each team member. A servant leader provides mentorship, guidance, and support to help their team members grow and reach their full potential. By investing in the growth and development of their team, servant leaders create a strong and capable workforce that can achieve great things together.

Overall, servant leadership is a powerful and effective management style that fosters trust, collaboration, and growth within a team. By putting the needs of others first and serving as a role model for their team, servant leaders create a positive and inclusive work environment where everyone can thrive. This approach is particularly well-suited for new managers who are looking to build strong and successful teams.

Characteristics of a Servant Leader

In the subchapter "Characteristics of a Servant Leader," new managers will learn about the key traits that define this unique leadership style. Servant leadership is a philosophy that puts the needs of others first and emphasizes serving the team rather than being served. It is a powerful and effective way to lead, as it fosters trust, collaboration, and a sense of purpose among team members.

One of the main characteristics of a servant leader is empathy. This means having the ability to understand and share the feelings of others, and to put oneself in their shoes. By showing empathy, a servant leader can build strong relationships with their team members and create a supportive and inclusive work environment.

Another important characteristic of a servant leader is humility. This involves setting aside one's ego and being willing to listen to others, admit mistakes, and learn from feedback. Humble leaders are open to different perspectives and are not afraid to ask for help when needed. This quality helps to create a culture of learning and growth within the team.

Servant leaders are also great communicators. They are able to clearly and effectively convey their vision, goals, and expectations to their team members. By keeping the lines of communication open, servant leaders ensure that everyone is on the same page and working towards a common purpose.

Additionally, servant leaders are committed to the growth and development of their team members. They provide support, guidance, and opportunities for learning and advancement. By investing in the personal and professional development of their team, servant leaders help to create a motivated and engaged workforce that is capable of achieving great things.

Overall, the characteristics of a servant leader include empathy, humility, effective communication, and a commitment to the growth and development of others. By embodying these traits, new managers can become more effective leaders and create a positive and productive work environment for their team.

Benefits of Servant Leadership

In this subchapter, we will explore the numerous benefits of adopting a servant leadership style as a new manager. Servant leadership is a management approach that focuses on serving others first, rather than being served. This style of leadership can greatly benefit both the leader and their team.

One of the key benefits of servant leadership is increased employee engagement. By prioritizing the needs and well-being of their team members, servant leaders create a positive work environment where employees feel valued and motivated. This, in turn, leads to higher levels of job satisfaction and productivity.

Another advantage of servant leadership is improved communication and collaboration within the team. Servant leaders are known for their ability to listen actively, communicate openly, and involve team members in decision-making processes. This fosters a sense of trust and respect among team members, leading to stronger relationships and better teamwork.

Servant leadership also promotes a culture of empathy and compassion in the workplace. By showing genuine care and concern for their team members, servant leaders create a supportive and nurturing environment where employees feel safe to take risks, make mistakes, and grow professionally. This can ultimately lead to higher levels of employee retention and loyalty.

Furthermore, servant leadership can enhance organizational performance and success. By focusing on the development and well-being of their team members, servant leaders can unlock the full potential of their employees and drive innovation and growth within the organization. This can result in increased profitability, customer satisfaction, and overall organizational effectiveness.

Adopting a servant leadership style can bring numerous benefits to both new managers and their teams. By prioritizing the needs of others, fostering a culture of collaboration and empathy, and driving organizational performance, servant leaders can create a positive and thriving work environment that benefits everyone involved. As a new manager, embracing servant leadership can set you apart as a compassionate and effective leader who truly cares about the success and well-being of your team.

Challenges of Implementing Servant Leadership

As new managers embark on their journey in implementing servant leadership, they are likely to face a number of challenges along the way. One of the main challenges is shifting from traditional management styles, such as autocratic or bureaucratic, to a more collaborative and empowering approach. This transition can be difficult for some managers who are used to being in control and making decisions on their own.

Another challenge of implementing servant leadership is the need for patience and trust in the process. Servant leadership requires a shift in mindset from focusing solely on results to also prioritizing the well-being and growth of team members. This can take time to see tangible results, and managers may need to have faith that their efforts will pay off in the long run.

Additionally, new managers may struggle with the concept of servant leadership in relation to other leadership styles, such as transformational or charismatic leadership. It can be challenging to find the right balance between being a servant leader who focuses on serving others, while also inspiring and motivating them to achieve their full potential.

Another challenge of implementing servant leadership is the fear of losing control. Some managers may feel uncomfortable relinquishing some of their power and authority in order to empower their team members. This fear can hinder their ability to fully embrace servant leadership and may prevent them from fully realizing the benefits of this approach.

Overall, the challenges of implementing servant leadership for new managers are numerous, but with dedication, patience, and a willingness to learn and grow, they can overcome these obstacles and become effective servant leaders who truly make a positive impact on their teams and organizations.

Developing a Servant Heart

In the world of management, there are various leadership styles that managers can adopt to guide their teams towards success. One such style that is gaining popularity is servant leadership. This style focuses on serving others first and leading by example, rather than exerting power and control over employees. Developing a servant heart is essential for new managers who want to effectively implement this style in their leadership approach.

To develop a servant heart, new managers must first understand the core principles of servant leadership. This includes putting the needs of others first, empathizing with their employees, and helping them grow and succeed. By embodying these principles, managers can create a positive and supportive work environment where employees feel valued and motivated to perform at their best.

Another important aspect of developing a servant heart is practicing humility. Servant leaders do not seek recognition or praise for their actions; instead, they focus on serving others selflessly and without expecting anything in return. By humbly serving their employees, new managers can build trust and foster strong relationships with their team members.

In addition to humility, new managers must also cultivate a sense of empathy and compassion towards their employees. Servant leaders listen actively to their team members, understand their perspectives, and offer support and guidance when needed. By showing empathy and compassion, managers can create a culture of trust and collaboration within their team.

Overall, developing a servant heart is essential for new managers who want to lead with compassion, humility, and empathy. By embodying the principles of servant leadership, managers can create a positive work environment where employees feel valued, supported, and motivated to achieve their goals. As new managers embark on their journey in servant leadership, they must remember that true leadership is not about power and control, but about serving others with kindness and humility.

Leading by Example

As a new manager, one of the most important aspects of your role is leading by example. Your team looks to you for guidance, support, and inspiration, and it is crucial that you set a positive example for them to follow. Leading with a servant heart means putting the needs of your team before your own, and demonstrating this through your actions is key to earning their trust and respect.

When it comes to management styles, there are a variety of approaches you can take. From autocratic to democratic, laissez-faire to transformational, each style has its own strengths and weaknesses. However, regardless of which style you choose to adopt, leading by example is essential. Showing your team that you are willing to roll up your sleeves and work alongside them, rather than simply giving orders from the sidelines, will go a long way in building a strong and cohesive team.

Servant leadership is a style that emphasizes empathy, humility, and a focus on serving others. By leading with a servant heart, you demonstrate to your team that you are there to support them, guide them, and help them succeed. This can create a more positive and productive work environment, as your team members feel valued and appreciated for their contributions.

In contrast, a bureaucratic management style relies heavily on rules, regulations, and hierarchy. While this style may work well in certain situations, it can also create a sense of rigidity and inflexibility within the team. By leading with a servant heart, you can help to soften the edges of a bureaucratic approach, and create a more human-centered and compassionate work environment.

In conclusion, no matter which management style you choose to adopt, leading by example is a crucial aspect of being an effective manager. By demonstrating empathy, humility, and a willingness to serve others, you can inspire your team to do the same. Leading with a servant heart is not always easy, but it is a powerful way to build trust, respect, and loyalty among your team members.

Building Trust and Empathy

Building Trust and Empathy is a crucial aspect of effective leadership, especially for new managers who are just starting out on their journey in the world of leadership. Trust is the foundation upon which strong relationships are built, and without trust, it is difficult to lead a team effectively. As a new manager, it is important to focus on building trust with your team members by being transparent, honest, and consistent in your actions and decisions.

Empathy is another key trait that new managers should cultivate in order to connect with their team members on a deeper level. By showing empathy towards others, new managers can better understand their team members' perspectives, feelings, and needs. This can help foster a sense of belonging and camaraderie within the team, leading to increased motivation and productivity.

When it comes to management styles, there are various approaches that new managers can adopt to build trust and empathy with their team members. The autocratic management style, which involves making decisions without consulting others, may not be the most effective in building trust and empathy. On the other hand, the democratic management style, which involves involving team members in decision-making processes, can help foster trust and empathy within the team.

The laissez-faire management style, which involves giving team members a high degree of autonomy, can also be effective in building trust and empathy, as it shows that the manager trusts and respects their team members' abilities. Transformational leadership, servant leadership, situational leadership, transactional leadership, charismatic leadership, bureaucratic management, and adaptive leadership are other styles that new managers can consider adopting to build trust and empathy with their team members.

In conclusion, building trust and empathy is essential for new managers looking to lead with a servant heart. By focusing on transparency, honesty, consistency, and empathy, new managers can build strong relationships with their team members and create a positive work environment that fosters collaboration, creativity, and productivity. By adopting the right management style that aligns with their values and goals, new managers can effectively build trust and empathy with their teams and become successful servant leaders.

Fostering a Collaborative Environment

As a new manager, it is important to understand the different management styles and how they can impact your team and workplace culture. One of the most effective ways to lead is through fostering a collaborative environment, where team members feel valued, heard, and empowered to contribute their ideas and expertise. By creating a culture of collaboration, you can harness the collective intelligence and creativity of your team to drive innovation and achieve shared goals.

The autocratic management style, characterized by top-down decision-making and strict control, can stifle collaboration and creativity within a team. In contrast, the democratic management style encourages open communication, participation, and shared decision-making, which can lead to increased trust and engagement among team members. By adopting a democratic approach, you can cultivate a culture of collaboration where everyone has a voice and feels invested in the team's success.

Similarly, the laissez-faire management style, where leaders take a hands-off approach and delegate responsibilities to team members, can promote autonomy and independence but may also lead to confusion and lack of direction. In contrast, the transformational leadership style focuses on inspiring and motivating team members to achieve their full potential, fostering a collaborative environment where individuals are encouraged to take risks and innovate.

Servant leadership, another effective management style, emphasizes serving others and putting the needs of the team first. By practicing empathy, active listening, and humility, servant leaders can build trust and create a collaborative environment where team members feel supported and valued. Additionally, situational leadership, transactional leadership, charismatic leadership, bureaucratic management, and adaptive leadership styles can all play a role in fostering collaboration within a team, depending on the specific needs and dynamics of the group.

In conclusion, as a new manager on a journey in servant leadership, it is important to understand the various management styles and how they can impact your team's ability to collaborate effectively. By fostering a collaborative environment where team members feel empowered, valued, and supported, you can harness the collective intelligence and creativity of your team to drive innovation and achieve shared goals. Embracing a servant leadership mindset, along with other effective management styles, can help you create a culture of collaboration that inspires and motivates your team to achieve greatness.

Encouraging Growth and Development

As new managers, it is essential to understand the different management styles available to you and how they can impact the growth and development of your team. Encouraging growth and development within your team is crucial for their success and the success of the organization as a whole. By recognizing the strengths and weaknesses of each management style, you can effectively lead your team towards achieving their full potential.

One common management style is the autocratic management style, where the manager makes decisions without input from their team. While this style can be effective in certain situations, it may hinder the growth and development of team members who thrive in collaborative environments. As a new manager, it is important to strike a balance between making decisions and empowering your team to contribute their ideas and expertise.

On the other hand, the democratic management style involves involving team members in decision-making processes. This style can be highly effective in encouraging growth and development, as it allows team members to feel valued and empowered. By fostering a culture of open communication and collaboration, you can create an environment where team members feel motivated to take on new challenges and grow in their roles.

Another management style to consider is the laissez-faire management style, where the manager takes a hands-off approach and allows team members to make decisions independently. While this style can be effective for self-motivated and experienced team members, it may not provide the necessary guidance and support for those who are still developing their skills. As a new manager, it is important to assess the needs of your team and adjust your management style accordingly to encourage their growth and development.

In conclusion, as a new manager, it is important to understand the various management styles available to you and how they can impact the growth and development of your team. By recognizing the strengths and weaknesses of each style, you can effectively lead your team towards achieving their full potential. By fostering a culture of open communication, collaboration, and empowerment, you can create an environment where team members feel motivated to take on new challenges and grow in their roles. Leading with a servant heart and a focus on encouraging growth and development will not only benefit your team but also contribute to the overall success of the organization.

Empowering Others

Empowering others is a key aspect of servant leadership that all new managers should strive to incorporate into their management style. By empowering others, managers are able to inspire and motivate their team members to reach their full potential. This not only benefits the individual team members but also contributes to the overall success of the team and organization.

One way to empower others is by adopting a democratic management style. This involves involving team members in decision-making processes and valuing their input and ideas. By giving team members a voice and allowing them to contribute to the decision-making process, managers can build trust and create a sense of ownership among team members, leading to increased motivation and engagement.

Another approach to empowering others is through transformational leadership. This leadership style focuses on inspiring and motivating team members to achieve their full potential and go above and beyond what is expected of them. Transformational leaders lead by example and inspire others through their vision and passion, creating a sense of purpose and direction that empowers team members to take on new challenges and strive for excellence.

Servant leadership is another effective way to empower others. This leadership style focuses on serving the needs of others and putting their interests first. By prioritizing the well-being and development of team members, servant leaders create a supportive and nurturing environment that empowers team members to grow and succeed. Servant leaders lead with humility and empathy, creating a culture of trust and collaboration that empowers team members to take risks and innovate.

In conclusion, empowering others is a crucial aspect of effective leadership that new managers should prioritize. By adopting a servant heart and focusing on empowering team members, managers can create a positive and empowering work environment that fosters growth and success. By incorporating elements of democratic, transformational, and servant leadership into their management style, new managers can inspire and motivate their team members to reach their full potential and achieve their goals.

Chapter 3: Applying Situational Leadership in Real-world Scenarios

Understanding Situational Leadership Theory

As a new manager, it is crucial to have a deep understanding of different management styles in order to effectively lead your team. One important theory that you should be familiar with is the Situational Leadership Theory. This theory, developed by Paul Hersey and Ken Blanchard in the 1970s, proposes that effective leaders are those who can adapt their style to suit the needs of their followers in different situations.

The Situational Leadership Theory is based on the idea that there is no one-size-fits-all approach to leadership. Instead, leaders must be flexible and able to adjust their leadership style depending on the readiness and ability of their followers. This means that a good leader must be able to assess the situation and determine the most appropriate leadership style to use in order to achieve the desired results.

There are four basic leadership styles in the Situational Leadership Theory: directing, coaching, supporting, and delegating. The directing style is appropriate for followers who lack the necessary skills and knowledge to perform a task, while the coaching style is used when followers have the skills but lack the confidence. The supporting style is used when followers have the confidence but need guidance, and the delegating style is used when followers are both skilled and confident.

By understanding the Situational Leadership Theory, new managers can become more effective leaders by being able to adapt their leadership style to suit the needs of their team members. This theory emphasizes the importance of being flexible and responsive to the situation at hand, which is crucial for achieving success in today's fast-paced business environment. As a new manager, it is important to familiarize yourself with the Situational Leadership Theory and practice applying its principles in your day-to-day interactions with your team.

Assessing Employee Readiness

Assessing employee readiness is a crucial step for new managers in determining the best approach to leading their team effectively. Understanding the readiness of your employees involves evaluating their skills, knowledge, and motivation to perform their job tasks successfully. By assessing employee readiness, managers can tailor their leadership style to meet the needs of their team members and ultimately drive better results.

One of the key management styles that can be used to assess employee readiness is the autocratic management style. This style involves making decisions without input from employees, which can be effective in certain situations where quick decision-making is needed. However, it may not be the best approach for assessing employee readiness as it does not allow for collaboration and input from team members.

On the other hand, the democratic management style involves including employees in the decision-making process, which can be beneficial for assessing employee readiness. By involving team members in decision-making, managers can gain valuable insights into their skills, knowledge, and motivation, which can help in determining the best course of action for leading the team effectively.

Another management style that can be used to assess employee readiness is the laissez-faire management style, which involves giving employees a high degree of autonomy in their work. While this approach can be effective for highly skilled and motivated employees, it may not be suitable for assessing employee readiness in all situations as it requires a high level of self-direction and motivation from team members.

Assessing employee readiness is a critical step for new managers in determining the best approach to leading their team effectively. By understanding the skills, knowledge, and motivation of their team members, managers can tailor their leadership style to meet the needs of their employees and ultimately drive better results. Whether using an autocratic, democratic, laissez-faire, or any other management style, it is important for new managers to assess employee readiness to ensure the success of their team.

Adapting Your Leadership Style

In the world of management, it is crucial for new managers to understand the importance of adapting their leadership style to fit the needs of their team and the situation at hand. Each management style has its own strengths and weaknesses, and knowing when to utilize each one can make a significant impact on the success of a team.

One of the most common management styles is the autocratic style, where the manager makes all decisions without input from their team. While this style can be effective in certain situations, it can also lead to low morale and productivity if not used appropriately. New managers should be aware of when to use this style and when to incorporate more democratic or servant leadership approaches to empower their team members.

Democratic management style, on the other hand, involves collaboration and input from team members when making decisions. This approach can lead to increased buy-in and commitment from employees, but it may not always be the most efficient or effective method in fast-paced environments. New managers should be prepared to balance this style with more hands-on approaches when necessary.

Laissez-faire management style is characterized by a hands-off approach, allowing team members to work independently with minimal supervision. While this style can foster creativity and autonomy, it can also lead to confusion and lack of direction if not managed properly. New managers should be mindful of when to step in and provide guidance to ensure that goals are being met.

In today's ever-changing business landscape, transformational leadership style is becoming increasingly popular. This approach involves inspiring and motivating team members to achieve a common goal, often through a shared vision and values. New managers should strive to embody this style by fostering a positive and dynamic work environment that encourages growth and innovation.

Ultimately, the key to effective leadership lies in adaptability. New managers should be open to incorporating various management styles, such as transactional, charismatic, bureaucratic, and adaptive leadership, based on the needs of their team and the situation at hand. By being flexible and willing to learn from experience, new managers can develop their own unique leadership style that resonates with their team members and drives success in their organization.

Providing Support and Guidance

As a new manager, one of the most important aspects of your role is providing support and guidance to your team members. This involves understanding their individual needs and helping them reach their full potential. In this subchapter, we will explore different management styles and how they can be leveraged to provide effective support and guidance to your team.

One management style that is often associated with providing support and guidance is servant leadership. Servant leaders prioritize the needs of their team members above their own, and strive to empower and develop their employees. By adopting a servant leadership style, you can build strong relationships with your team members and create a supportive work environment where everyone can thrive.

Another management style that focuses on providing support and guidance is transformational leadership. Transformational leaders inspire and motivate their team members to achieve their goals, and are able to guide them through challenges and setbacks. By embracing a transformational leadership style, you can help your team members grow and develop both personally and professionally.

On the other end of the spectrum, autocratic management style, which involves making decisions without input from team members, can hinder your ability to provide effective support and guidance. While there may be instances where autocratic leadership is necessary, it is important to strike a balance between making decisions and involving your team in the decision-making process.

As a new manager, it is crucial to understand the different management styles and how they can impact your ability to provide support and guidance to your team. By adopting a servant or transformational leadership style, you can create a supportive work environment where your team members can thrive and reach their full potential. Remember to consider the individual needs of your team members and tailor your approach accordingly to best support and guide them in their roles.

Delegating Responsibilities

As a new manager, one of the most important skills you can develop is the ability to delegate responsibilities effectively. Delegating tasks to your team members not only helps you manage your workload more efficiently, but it also empowers your team to take ownership of their work and develop their skills and abilities. In this subchapter, we will explore the various management styles and how they relate to delegation.

Autocratic management style is characterized by a top-down approach where decisions are made by the manager without input from the team. While this style can be effective in certain situations, it can hinder the delegation process as team members may feel disempowered and undervalued. As a new manager, it is important to strike a balance between making decisions and involving your team in the process.

On the other end of the spectrum is the democratic management style, where decisions are made collectively by the team. This style promotes collaboration and teamwork, making it easier to delegate responsibilities as team members are more likely to take ownership of their tasks. However, it is important to ensure that the delegation process is still structured and organized to avoid confusion and miscommunication.

Laissez-faire management style is characterized by a hands-off approach, where the manager provides minimal guidance and oversight. While this style can promote autonomy and creativity among team members, it can also lead to a lack of accountability and direction. As a new manager, it is important to find a balance between giving your team space to work independently and providing support when needed.

Transformational leadership style focuses on inspiring and motivating team members to achieve their full potential. This style encourages managers to delegate responsibilities based on individual strengths and abilities, allowing team members to grow and develop in their roles. By adopting a transformational leadership style, you can create a positive and empowering work environment where delegation is seen as a tool for personal and professional growth.

Communicating Effectively

Communicating effectively is a crucial skill for new managers to develop in order to lead with a servant heart. In the world of management styles, effective communication can make or break a team's success. Understanding the different management styles, such as autocratic, democratic, laissez-faire, transformational, servant, situational, transactional, charismatic, bureaucratic, and adaptive, is key to knowing how to effectively communicate with your team.

One of the most common management styles is autocratic, where the manager makes decisions without consulting their team. In this style, communication may be one-way, with little room for feedback or input from team members. As a new manager, it is important to recognize when this style may be necessary, but also to understand the importance of open communication and collaboration in fostering a positive work environment.

On the other end of the spectrum is the democratic management style, where decisions are made collectively with input from team members. In this style, communication is key to ensuring that everyone's voice is heard and that decisions are made with the best interests of the team in mind. As a servant leader, it is important to foster an environment of open communication and collaboration to empower your team members and make them feel valued.

Laissez-faire management style is characterized by a hands-off approach, allowing team members to make decisions independently. While this style can be effective in certain situations, effective communication is still essential to ensure that team members have the support and guidance they need to succeed. As a new manager, it is important to strike a balance between giving your team autonomy and providing the necessary guidance and support through effective communication.

Effective communication is a cornerstone of servant leadership and is essential for new managers to master in order to lead with a servant heart. By understanding the different management styles and their implications for communication, new managers can cultivate an environment of trust, collaboration, and empowerment within their teams. By honing their communication skills, new managers can build strong relationships with their team members and inspire them to achieve their full potential.

Handling Conflict and Challenges

As new managers, it is important to understand that conflict and challenges are inevitable in any leadership role. How we handle these situations can greatly impact our team and the overall success of the organization. In this subchapter, we will explore various management styles and how they can be applied when facing conflict and challenges.

One of the most common management styles is the autocratic management style, where the manager makes decisions without consulting others. While this style can be effective in certain situations, it can also lead to resentment and lack of motivation among team members. When faced with conflict, autocratic managers may need to consider a more collaborative approach to find a solution that works for everyone involved.

On the other hand, the democratic management style involves involving team members in decision-making processes. This can be beneficial when dealing with conflict, as it allows for different perspectives to be considered and can lead to more creative solutions. New managers who adopt this style may find that their team is more engaged and motivated to overcome challenges together.

Laissez-faire management style, where managers give employees a high degree of freedom to make decisions, can also be effective in handling conflict. By trusting their team to find solutions on their own, managers can encourage autonomy and innovation. However, it is important for managers to provide support and guidance when needed to ensure that conflicts are resolved in a timely manner.

Transformational leadership style focuses on inspiring and motivating team members to achieve a common goal. When faced with conflict, transformational leaders can use their charisma and vision to rally their team and find creative solutions. By emphasizing teamwork and collaboration, new managers can effectively manage conflict and challenges in a way that brings out the best in their team.

Servant leadership style, which prioritizes the needs of others and focuses on serving the team, can also be a powerful tool in handling conflict. By putting the needs of team members first, new managers can build trust and create a positive work environment where conflicts can be resolved peacefully. By adopting a servant leadership approach, managers can lead by example and inspire their team to work together towards common goals.

Evaluating Performance

Evaluating performance is a critical aspect of effective leadership for new managers. It involves assessing the performance of team members and providing feedback to help them improve and grow. Each management style has its own approach to evaluating performance, and it is important for new managers to understand the differences in order to choose the most appropriate method for their team.

Autocratic management style typically involves a top-down approach where the manager makes all decisions and closely monitors the performance of team members. When evaluating performance, autocratic managers may focus on strict adherence to rules and procedures, as well as individual productivity. Feedback is often given in a directive manner, with little room for discussion or input from team members.

In contrast, democratic management style emphasizes collaboration and participation in decision-making. When evaluating performance, democratic managers may seek input from team members and encourage open communication. Feedback is often given in a constructive and inclusive manner, with a focus on empowering team members to take ownership of their performance and growth.

Laissez-faire management style allows team members a high degree of autonomy and flexibility in how they approach their work. When evaluating performance, laissez-faire managers may focus on overall outcomes and results rather than micromanaging the process. Feedback is often given in a hands-off manner, with an emphasis on trusting team members to take responsibility for their own performance.

Transformational leadership style focuses on inspiring and motivating team members to achieve their full potential. When evaluating performance, transformational leaders may focus on personal development and growth, as well as aligning individual goals with the overall vision of the organization. Feedback is often given in a motivational and inspiring manner, with an emphasis on recognizing and rewarding achievements.

Servant leadership style emphasizes serving the needs of others and putting the interests of team members first. When evaluating performance, servant leaders may focus on understanding the individual strengths and challenges of team members, as well as providing support and guidance to help them succeed. Feedback is often given in a compassionate and empathetic manner, with an emphasis on building trust and fostering a positive work environment.

Continuous Improvement and Adaptation

As a new manager, it is essential to understand the importance of continuous improvement and adaptation in order to be successful in today's fast-paced business environment. In the ever-changing landscape of management styles, it is crucial to be flexible and open to new ideas in order to stay ahead of the competition and effectively lead your team.

One of the key aspects of continuous improvement is the ability to adapt your management style to meet the needs of your team and the organization as a whole. Different situations may require different approaches, and as a manager, it is important to be able to recognize when a change in leadership style is necessary. By being open to feedback and willing to make adjustments as needed, you can create a more positive and productive work environment for your team.

In the realm of management styles, there are several different approaches that managers can take to lead their teams. From autocratic and bureaucratic management styles to democratic and laissez-faire management styles, each approach has its own strengths and weaknesses. As a new manager, it is important to familiarize yourself with the various management styles and understand when each style may be most effective in a given situation.

In addition to traditional management styles, new managers should also be aware of more modern approaches to leadership, such as transformational, servant, situational, transactional, charismatic, and adaptive leadership styles. These styles focus on building relationships, empowering employees, and adapting to changing circumstances in order to achieve success. By incorporating elements of these styles into your own leadership approach, you can become a more effective and dynamic manager.

Continuous improvement and adaptation are essential components of effective leadership. By staying open to new ideas, being willing to make changes when necessary, and incorporating elements of different management styles into your leadership approach, you can become a more well-rounded and successful manager. Remember, the key to success in leadership is not to find one style that works best, but to be able to adapt and evolve as needed in order to meet the ever-changing demands of the business world.

Chapter 4: Integrating Adaptive Leadership into Your Management Approach

The Concept of Adaptive Leadership

Adaptive leadership is a concept that is gaining traction in the world of management styles. As a new manager, it is important to understand the principles behind adaptive leadership and how it can be applied in your role. Adaptive leadership is all about being able to respond to changing circumstances and environments. It requires flexibility, creativity, and openness to new ideas.

One of the key aspects of adaptive leadership is the ability to embrace uncertainty and ambiguity. In today's fast-paced and constantly evolving business world, it is crucial for managers to be comfortable with not having all the answers. Adaptive leaders are able to navigate through complex situations and make decisions in the face of uncertainty.

Another important aspect of adaptive leadership is the willingness to challenge the status quo. Adaptive leaders are not afraid to question existing practices and ways of thinking. They are open to new perspectives and are willing to experiment with different approaches in order to achieve their goals.

Adaptive leadership also involves a strong focus on building relationships and fostering collaboration. As a new manager, it is important to recognize the value of teamwork and collective problem-solving. Adaptive leaders encourage open communication and collaboration among team members, which can lead to more innovative solutions and better outcomes.

Adaptive leadership is a valuable concept for new managers to understand and embrace. By being flexible, open-minded, and willing to challenge the status quo, you can become a more effective leader in today's ever-changing business landscape. Embracing adaptive leadership can help you navigate through uncertainty, build strong relationships, and ultimately achieve success in your role as a manager.

Embracing Change and Uncertainty

In the world of management, change and uncertainty are inevitable. As a new manager, it is crucial to embrace these challenges with an open mind and a servant heart. While it may be tempting to stick to a rigid management style, such as autocratic or bureaucratic, it is important to recognize that flexibility and adaptability are key in today's fast-paced business environment.

One of the most effective ways to navigate change and uncertainty is to adopt a transformational leadership style. This approach focuses on inspiring and motivating employees to reach their full potential, even in the face of uncertainty. By fostering a sense of trust and empowerment within your team, you can create a culture of resilience and innovation that can weather any storm.

Another valuable tool for managing change and uncertainty is servant leadership. This style emphasizes putting the needs of others first and leading by example. By serving your team with humility and compassion, you can build strong relationships and create a sense of unity that will help your team navigate through uncertain times.

Situational leadership is also a useful approach when facing change and uncertainty. This style involves adapting your leadership style to fit the specific needs of each situation or team member. By being flexible and responsive to changing circumstances, you can effectively guide your team through periods of transition and uncertainty.

As a new manager, it is essential to embrace change and uncertainty with a servant heart. By adopting a transformational or servant leadership style, practicing situational leadership, and remaining open to new ideas and approaches, you can successfully navigate through the challenges of managing in a rapidly changing world. Remember, change is inevitable, but with the right mindset and leadership style, you can turn uncertainty into opportunity.

Navigating Complex Situations

Navigating complex situations is a crucial skill for new managers to develop as they embark on their journey in servant leadership. Understanding different management styles is essential in order to effectively address the diverse challenges that may arise in the workplace. From autocratic and democratic management styles to transformational and servant leadership styles, each approach offers unique benefits and challenges that new managers must navigate.

Autocratic management style is characterized by a top-down approach where the manager makes decisions without input from subordinates. While this style can be efficient in certain situations, it can also lead to disengagement and resentment among employees. New managers must be mindful of when to employ this style and when to seek input from their team in order to foster a more collaborative work environment.

On the other hand, democratic management style encourages participation and input from team members in decision-making processes. This approach can lead to greater employee satisfaction and engagement, but may also result in slower decision-making. New managers must strike a balance between empowering their team members and maintaining efficiency in order to effectively navigate complex situations.

Laissez-faire management style involves giving employees a high degree of autonomy and freedom to make decisions. While this approach can foster creativity and innovation, it can also lead to confusion and lack of direction if not implemented effectively. New managers must provide clear expectations and support to their team members in order to successfully navigate complex situations using this management style.

Transformational leadership style focuses on inspiring and motivating employees to achieve their full potential. This approach can be highly effective in driving organizational change and growth, but requires strong communication and relationship-building skills. New managers must lead by example and cultivate a culture of trust and collaboration in order to effectively navigate complex situations using this leadership style.

Building Resilience and Flexibility

Building resilience and flexibility is crucial for new managers as they navigate the challenges of leading a team effectively. In today's fast-paced and constantly changing work environment, the ability to adapt to unforeseen circumstances and bounce back from setbacks is a valuable skill that can set a manager apart from their peers. In this subchapter, we will explore how new managers can cultivate resilience and flexibility in their leadership approach to better serve their teams and achieve organizational goals.

One of the key aspects of building resilience and flexibility as a new manager is to embrace a growth mindset. This mindset acknowledges that failures and setbacks are opportunities for learning and growth, rather than reasons for giving up. By fostering a culture of continuous improvement and encouraging team members to take risks and learn from their mistakes, new managers can create a more resilient and adaptable team that can thrive in the face of challenges.

Another important aspect of building resilience and flexibility is the ability to effectively manage change. In today's dynamic work environment, new managers must be prepared to navigate unexpected changes and disruptions with grace and composure. By communicating openly and transparently with their team members, new managers can help alleviate fears and uncertainties that may arise during times of change, fostering a sense of trust and collaboration that can help the team weather any storm.

Furthermore, new managers can enhance their resilience and flexibility by developing strong relationships with their team members. By fostering a sense of camaraderie and mutual respect within the team, new managers can create a support system that can help them navigate challenges and setbacks more effectively. By empowering team members to take ownership of their work and providing them with the resources and support they need to succeed, new managers can cultivate a more resilient and adaptable team that can thrive in any situation.

Building resilience and flexibility is a critical skill for new managers to develop as they embark on their journey in servant leadership. By embracing a growth mindset, effectively managing change, and fostering strong relationships with their team members, new managers can create a more resilient and adaptable team that can thrive in today's fast-paced and ever-changing work environment. By incorporating these principles into their leadership approach, new managers can become more effective leaders who can inspire and empower their teams to achieve greatness.

Encouraging Innovation and Creativity

As a new manager, it is essential to understand the importance of encouraging innovation and creativity within your team. These qualities are key to driving growth, fostering a positive work environment, and ultimately achieving success in your role as a leader. In this subchapter, we will explore how different management styles can either hinder or promote innovation and creativity within your team.

Autocratic management style, characterized by top-down decision-making and strict control, often stifles innovation and creativity. By dictating all decisions and processes, this style leaves little room for employees to think outside the box or contribute their unique ideas. As a new manager, it is crucial to recognize the limitations of this approach and instead embrace more collaborative styles that empower your team to innovate and be creative.

On the other end of the spectrum, the democratic management style encourages participation and input from all team members. By fostering a culture of open communication and shared decision-making, this style can lead to increased innovation and creativity within your team. As a new manager, consider implementing practices that allow for brainstorming sessions, idea sharing, and feedback loops to encourage creativity and innovation among your team members.

The laissez-faire management style, characterized by a hands-off approach and minimal direction from the manager, can also promote innovation and creativity within a team. By giving employees the freedom to explore new ideas and solutions independently, this style can lead to fresh perspectives and innovative solutions. However, it is essential for new managers to strike a balance between providing autonomy and guidance to ensure that creativity is channeled effectively towards achieving team goals.

Transformational leadership style, characterized by inspiring and motivating employees to reach their full potential, is another effective way to encourage innovation and creativity within your team. By setting a compelling vision, fostering a culture of continuous learning and growth, and recognizing and rewarding innovative ideas, you can inspire your team to think creatively and push boundaries. As a new manager, consider adopting a transformational leadership style to unlock the full potential of your team and drive innovation in your organization.

Leading Through Crisis

In times of crisis, effective leadership is crucial to navigate through challenges and lead a team towards success. As a new manager, it is important to understand the different management styles and how they can be applied in times of crisis. One such management style is servant leadership, which focuses on putting the needs of others first and empowering team members to reach their full potential. By leading with a servant heart, new managers can build trust, inspire loyalty, and create a positive work environment even in the midst of uncertainty.

Autocratic management style, on the other hand, involves making decisions without consulting team members and is often seen as authoritative. While this style may be effective in certain situations, it can create a sense of fear and resentment among team members during a crisis. A more democratic management style, which involves involving team members in decision-making processes, can foster collaboration, innovation, and a sense of ownership among team members. By allowing team members to have a voice in how to tackle challenges, new managers can build a stronger, more resilient team.

Laissez-faire management style, where managers take a hands-off approach and provide little direction to team members, may not be the most effective during a crisis. In times of uncertainty, team members may feel lost and unsupported without clear guidance and direction. Instead, new managers can consider adopting a transformational leadership style, which focuses on inspiring and motivating team members to achieve their goals. By setting a clear vision, providing support, and encouraging growth, new managers can empower their team to overcome obstacles and thrive in challenging times.

In addition to servant leadership and transformational leadership styles, new managers can also consider situational leadership, transactional leadership, charismatic leadership, bureaucratic management, and adaptive leadership styles when leading through a crisis. Each of these styles offers unique strengths and can be effective depending on the specific circumstances and needs of the team. By understanding the different management styles and how they can be applied in times of crisis, new managers can develop a flexible and adaptable approach to leadership that will help them navigate challenges and lead their team to success.

Engaging Stakeholders

Engaging stakeholders is a crucial aspect of effective leadership, regardless of the management style being employed. As a new manager, it is important to understand the different types of stakeholders that may be involved in your organization and how to effectively communicate and collaborate with them. By engaging stakeholders in a meaningful way, you can build trust, foster positive relationships, and ultimately drive success for your team and organization.

In an autocratic management style, where decision-making power is centralized with the manager, engaging stakeholders may be challenging. However, it is still important to seek feedback and input from key stakeholders to ensure their needs and concerns are being addressed. By involving stakeholders in the decision-making process, even in a limited capacity, you can demonstrate your commitment to transparency and accountability.

On the other end of the spectrum, in a democratic management style, engaging stakeholders is key to fostering a collaborative and inclusive environment. By soliciting input from a wide range of stakeholders, such as employees, customers, and community members, you can gather diverse perspectives and ideas that can lead to more informed decision-making and better outcomes for your organization.

In a laissez-faire management style, where employees are given a high degree of autonomy, engaging stakeholders may involve providing them with the resources and support they need to thrive. By actively listening to their feedback and addressing any concerns or challenges they may have, you can create a more supportive and empowering work environment that encourages innovation and growth.

Regardless of the management style you choose to adopt, engaging stakeholders in a meaningful way is essential for building strong relationships and driving success. By demonstrating a commitment to collaboration, transparency, and accountability, you can create a positive and inclusive culture that empowers your team and organization to achieve their goals. Remember, leadership is not about being in control, but rather about empowering others to succeed.

Embracing Diversity and Inclusion

As a new manager, it is crucial to understand the importance of embracing diversity and inclusion in the workplace. In today's globalized world, organizations are made up of individuals from various backgrounds, cultures, and experiences. Embracing diversity means recognizing and valuing these differences, while inclusion means creating an environment where everyone feels welcome and respected.

One management style that aligns well with embracing diversity and inclusion is servant leadership. Servant leaders prioritize the needs of their team members and work to create a supportive and inclusive work environment. By focusing on the well-being and development of their employees, servant leaders can foster a culture of respect and collaboration.

In contrast, autocratic management style, which is characterized by top-down decision-making and strict control over employees, may hinder diversity and inclusion efforts. Employees may feel marginalized and undervalued in an autocratic environment, leading to decreased morale and productivity. As a new manager, it is important to recognize the limitations of this management style and consider alternative approaches that promote diversity and inclusion.

Another management style that can support diversity and inclusion is transformational leadership. Transformational leaders inspire and motivate their team members to achieve their full potential, while also promoting a culture of openness and inclusivity. By encouraging creativity and innovation, transformational leaders can create a dynamic and diverse work environment where all employees feel empowered to contribute their unique perspectives.

In conclusion, as a new manager, it is essential to adopt a leadership style that embraces diversity and inclusion. By prioritizing the well-being of your team members, fostering a culture of respect and collaboration, and encouraging creativity and innovation, you can create a workplace where everyone feels valued and respected. Embracing diversity and inclusion is not only the right thing to do, but it also leads to increased productivity, employee satisfaction, and overall success for your organization.

Enhancing Organizational Agility

As new managers, it is crucial to understand the importance of enhancing organizational agility in today's rapidly changing business environment. Organizational agility refers to the ability of a company to quickly adapt to changes, seize opportunities, and respond to challenges in a timely and effective manner. In order to enhance organizational agility, new managers must be willing to embrace different management styles and leadership approaches that promote flexibility, innovation, and resilience.

One of the key management styles that can help enhance organizational agility is the democratic management style. This approach involves involving employees in decision-making processes, encouraging collaboration, and empowering teams to take ownership of their work. By fostering a culture of open communication and shared responsibility, new managers can facilitate quicker decision-making and problem-solving, leading to increased agility and adaptability within the organization.

Another effective leadership style for enhancing organizational agility is transformational leadership. This approach focuses on inspiring and motivating employees to achieve their full potential, fostering creativity and innovation, and promoting a culture of continuous learning and improvement. By encouraging employees to think outside the box, take risks, and embrace change, new managers can help build a more agile and resilient organization that can quickly respond to new opportunities and challenges.

In addition to embracing different management styles and leadership approaches, new managers can also enhance organizational agility by fostering a culture of servant leadership. This approach emphasizes empathy, humility, and a focus on serving others, rather than exerting power and control. By leading with a servant heart, new managers can create a more inclusive and collaborative work environment, where employees feel valued, supported, and empowered to take on new challenges and opportunities.

Overall, enhancing organizational agility requires new managers to be open-minded, flexible, and willing to adapt to changing circumstances. By embracing different management styles, leadership approaches, and organizational cultures that promote flexibility, innovation, and resilience, new managers can help build a more agile and responsive organization that is better equipped to thrive in today's fast-paced and unpredictable business environment.

Sustaining Long-term Success

Sustaining long-term success as a new manager requires a deep understanding of various management styles and how they can impact your team's performance. One of the most common management styles is the autocratic style, where the manager makes all the decisions without consulting their team. While this style can be effective in certain situations, it can also lead to resentment and lower morale among team members.

On the other hand, the democratic management style involves actively involving team members in decision-making processes. This can lead to higher levels of engagement and innovation, as team members feel empowered and valued. However, it can also slow down decision-making processes and may not always be suitable for quick-paced environments.

The laissez-faire management style, on the other hand, involves giving team members a high degree of autonomy and freedom to make decisions. While this can foster a sense of ownership and responsibility among team members, it can also lead to confusion and lack of direction if not implemented effectively.

As a new manager, it is important to understand the strengths and weaknesses of each management style and adapt your approach based on the specific needs of your team and the situation at hand. Transformational leadership, for example, involves inspiring and motivating team members to achieve a common goal. This style can be highly effective in driving organizational change and fostering a culture of innovation.

Servant leadership, on the other hand, focuses on serving the needs of others and empowering team members to reach their full potential. This approach can lead to higher levels of trust and collaboration within the team, ultimately leading to sustainable long-term success. By understanding and leveraging different management styles, new managers can effectively navigate the complex challenges of leadership and create a positive and productive work environment for their team.

Chapter 5: Becoming a Well-rounded Leader in the Modern Workplace

In the fast-paced world of management, it is crucial for new managers to understand and balance different leadership styles in order to effectively lead their teams. Each leadership style has its own strengths and weaknesses, and knowing when to utilize each one can make a significant impact on the success of a team.

Balancing Different Leadership Styles

One common leadership style is the autocratic management style, where the manager makes decisions without input from their team members. While this style can be effective in certain situations, it can also lead to feelings of resentment and lack of motivation among team members. New managers should be cautious when using this style and consider seeking input from their team to foster a more collaborative environment.

On the other end of the spectrum is the democratic management style, where decisions are made collectively with input from all team members. This style can lead to increased employee engagement and buy-in, but it can also be time-consuming and inefficient. New managers should consider using this style when seeking input and buy-in from their team is important for the success of a project.

The laissez-faire management style is characterized by a hands-off approach, where the manager provides little to no direction to their team. While this style can empower team members to take ownership of their work, it can also lead to confusion and lack of accountability. New managers should use this style sparingly and provide clear expectations and support to ensure the success of their team.

Transformational leadership is a style that inspires and motivates team members to achieve their full potential. This style focuses on building relationships and empowering team members to reach their goals. New managers should strive to incorporate elements of transformational leadership into their own style to foster a positive and empowering work environment. By balancing different leadership styles, new managers can create a dynamic and effective team that is equipped to tackle any challenge that comes their way.

Developing Your Personal Leadership Philosophy

As a new manager, it is important to take the time to develop your personal leadership philosophy. Your leadership philosophy is the foundation upon which you will build your management style and approach to leading others. By taking the time to reflect on your values, beliefs, and goals, you can create a clear and compelling vision for how you want to lead your team.

There are many different management styles to choose from, each with its own strengths and weaknesses. Some managers may prefer an autocratic management style, where decisions are made quickly and without input from others. Others may lean towards a democratic management style, where team members are actively involved in decision-making processes. Laissez-faire managers may take a more hands-off approach, allowing team members to work independently.

One popular leadership style is transformational leadership, which focuses on inspiring and motivating team members to achieve their full potential. Servant leadership is another style that prioritizes the needs of others above all else. Situational leadership, on the other hand, involves adapting your leadership style to fit the needs of the situation at hand.

Transactional leadership focuses on creating clear expectations and rewards for team members, while charismatic leadership relies on the leader's personality and charisma to inspire others. Bureaucratic management may be necessary in certain situations where strict rules and procedures are required. Adaptive leadership is all about being flexible and responsive to changing circumstances.

Ultimately, the key to developing your personal leadership philosophy is to align it with your values and beliefs. By staying true to yourself and leading with authenticity, you can inspire trust and loyalty in your team. Remember that there is no one-size-fits-all approach to leadership, so take the time to explore different styles and find what works best for you. With a clear and well-defined leadership philosophy, you can confidently navigate the challenges of management and lead your team to success.

Seeking Feedback and Continuous Learning

As new managers, seeking feedback and continuously learning is crucial in developing your leadership skills and abilities. In the world of management styles, there are various approaches that you can adopt, each with its own unique characteristics and benefits. By understanding these different styles, you can better tailor your leadership approach to suit the needs of your team and organization.

One common management style is the autocratic management style, where decisions are made by the manager without input from the team. While this style can be effective in certain situations, it can also lead to feelings of resentment and disengagement among team members. As a new manager, it is important to seek feedback from your team to ensure that your leadership style is effective and well-received.

On the other hand, the democratic management style involves collaboration and input from team members in decision-making processes. This style can lead to increased engagement and buy-in from employees, as they feel like their voices are being heard. By seeking feedback from your team and allowing them to contribute to decision-making processes, you can foster a culture of trust and empowerment within your organization.

In contrast, the laissez-faire management style involves giving employees a high degree of autonomy and freedom in how they approach their work. While this style can be beneficial in fostering creativity and innovation, it can also lead to a lack of direction and accountability. By seeking feedback from your team on their preferred level of autonomy and support, you can strike a balance that allows for both independence and guidance.

As you continue on your journey in servant leadership, it is important to remember that leadership is a journey of continuous learning and growth. By seeking feedback from your team and actively soliciting input on your leadership style, you can adapt and evolve as a leader to better serve your team and organization. Remember, leadership is not about having all the answers, but rather about being open to feedback and willing to learn from those around you.

Building a Support Network

As a new manager, one of the most important things you can do for yourself is to build a strong support network. This network can consist of mentors, colleagues, friends, and even family members who can provide you with guidance, advice, and a listening ear when you need it most. Having a support network in place can help you navigate the challenges of leadership and ensure that you have the resources you need to succeed.

When it comes to management styles, there are many different approaches you can take. Some managers prefer to take a more autocratic approach, making decisions without input from their team members. While this style can be effective in certain situations, it can also lead to resentment and a lack of buy-in from your employees. On the other end of the spectrum is the democratic management style, where decisions are made collectively with input from all team members. This approach can foster a sense of ownership and empowerment among your team, but it can also be time-consuming and inefficient.

Another management style to consider is the laissez-faire approach, where managers take a hands-off approach and allow their team members to make decisions independently. While this style can be effective with a highly skilled and motivated team, it can also lead to confusion and lack of direction if not implemented properly. One of the most effective management styles is transformational leadership, where managers inspire and motivate their team members to achieve their full potential. This approach can help create a positive and productive work environment, but it requires strong communication and interpersonal skills.

Servant leadership is another popular management style that focuses on serving the needs of others before your own. This approach can help build trust and loyalty among your team members, but it can also be challenging to implement if you are used to more traditional leadership styles. Situational leadership is a flexible approach that involves adapting your leadership style to the specific needs of your team and the situation at hand. This style can be effective in a variety of situations, but it requires a deep understanding of your team members and their strengths and weaknesses.

No matter what management style you choose, it's important to remember that building a support network is key to your success as a new manager. Surrounding yourself with people who can provide you with guidance, feedback, and support can help you navigate the challenges of leadership and ensure that you are able to lead with confidence and compassion. By building a strong support network, you can set yourself up for success and become the kind of leader that inspires and motivates others to reach their full potential.

Leading with Integrity and Authenticity

In the realm of leadership, integrity and authenticity are two key qualities that can make or break a manager's success. Leading with integrity means consistently doing what is right, even when no one is watching. It involves being honest, ethical, and transparent in all interactions and decision-making processes. Authenticity, on the other hand, involves being true to oneself and leading in a way that is genuine and sincere. When a manager leads with integrity and authenticity, they build trust, credibility, and respect among their team members.

When it comes to management styles, those who lead with integrity and authenticity often gravitate towards servant leadership. Servant leaders prioritize the needs of their team members above their own, and they lead by example, demonstrating humility, empathy, and a commitment to serving others. This style of leadership fosters a positive and empowering work environment where team members feel valued and supported. New managers can benefit greatly from adopting a servant leadership approach, as it can help them build strong relationships with their team members and inspire them to do their best work.

In contrast, autocratic management style, which is characterized by top-down decision-making and a lack of input from team members, can be detrimental to a manager's reputation if not executed with integrity and authenticity. While there may be times when a more directive approach is necessary, it is important for managers to communicate openly and honestly with their team members about the reasons behind their decisions. By leading with integrity and authenticity, even autocratic managers can earn the trust and respect of their team members.

Similarly, democratic management style, which involves seeking input from team members and making decisions collaboratively, can be highly effective when coupled with integrity and authenticity. By actively listening to their team members, valuing their opinions, and involving them in the decision-making process, managers can create a culture of transparency, inclusivity, and trust within their team. This approach can lead to increased employee engagement, motivation, and satisfaction, ultimately driving better results for the organization.

Leading with integrity and authenticity is essential for new managers looking to establish themselves as effective and respected leaders. By embracing servant leadership principles and prioritizing the needs of their team members, managers can create a positive work environment where trust, respect, and collaboration thrive. Whether they choose to adopt a democratic, autocratic, laissez-faire, or any other management style, new managers can benefit greatly from incorporating integrity and authenticity into their leadership approach. By doing so, they can build strong relationships with their team members, inspire trust and loyalty, and drive success for their organization.

Inspiring and Motivating Others

As a new manager, one of the most important skills you can develop is the ability to inspire and motivate others. In order to be an effective leader, you must be able to rally your team around a common goal and encourage them to give their best effort. This subchapter will explore different strategies and techniques for inspiring and motivating others, regardless of your management style.

One of the key aspects of inspiring and motivating others is leading by example. As a new manager, your team will look to you for guidance and direction. By demonstrating a strong work ethic, positive attitude, and commitment to the team's goals, you can inspire your employees to do the same. Remember, actions speak louder than words, so make sure your behavior aligns with the values and expectations you have for your team.

Another important aspect of inspiring and motivating others is recognizing and celebrating their achievements. Everyone likes to feel appreciated and valued for their contributions, so be sure to acknowledge your team members' hard work and accomplishments. This can be as simple as a verbal thank you or as elaborate as a team outing or award ceremony. By showing your team that their efforts are noticed and appreciated, you can boost morale and motivation.

In addition to recognizing achievements, it's also important to provide regular feedback and encouragement. As a new manager, it can be easy to get caught up in the day-to-day tasks and forget to check in with your team members. However, taking the time to provide constructive feedback and words of encouragement can make a big difference in their motivation and performance. Regular communication and support can help your team members feel valued and motivated to continue striving for excellence.

Lastly, consider incorporating elements of servant leadership into your management style. Servant leaders prioritize the needs of others above their own, and work to empower and support their team members. By adopting a servant leadership approach, you can create a culture of trust, collaboration, and mutual respect within your team. This can lead to increased motivation, engagement, and overall success for both you and your employees. As a new manager, embracing the principles of servant leadership can help you build strong, cohesive teams that are capable of achieving great things.

Cultivating a Positive Work Culture

Cultivating a positive work culture is essential for any new manager looking to lead with a servant heart. A positive work culture can lead to increased employee engagement, higher productivity, and lower turnover rates. It is important for new managers to understand the different management styles and how they can impact the work culture within their team.

One management style that can help cultivate a positive work culture is the democratic management style. This style involves involving employees in decision-making processes and valuing their input. By giving employees a voice in the decision-making process, new managers can empower their team members and create a sense of ownership within the team.

Another management style that can contribute to a positive work culture is the transformational leadership style. Transformational leaders inspire and motivate their team members to achieve their full potential. By focusing on individual growth and development, new managers can create a culture of continuous improvement within their team.

Servant leadership is another management style that can help new managers cultivate a positive work culture. Servant leaders prioritize the needs of their team members and work to support their growth and development. By putting the needs of their team first, new managers can create a culture of collaboration and mutual respect within their team.

In conclusion, new managers looking to cultivate a positive work culture should consider incorporating elements of democratic, transformational, and servant leadership styles into their management approach. By valuing employee input, focusing on individual growth and development, and prioritizing the needs of their team members, new managers can create a work culture that is conducive to success and growth. By leading with a servant heart, new managers can inspire their team members to reach their full potential and achieve their goals.

Embracing the Journey of Leadership Growth

As new managers embark on their leadership journey, it is essential for them to embrace the process of growth and development. Leadership is not a destination, but rather a journey of continuous learning and improvement. By understanding and embracing the journey of leadership growth, new managers can become more effective and influential leaders within their organizations.

One of the key aspects of embracing the journey of leadership growth is understanding the various management styles that exist. From autocratic and democratic management styles to laissez-faire and transformational leadership styles, each approach offers unique strengths and weaknesses. By familiarizing themselves with these different styles, new managers can better adapt their leadership approach to different situations and individuals.

Among the various management styles, servant leadership stands out as a particularly impactful and effective approach. This style emphasizes empathy, humility, and a focus on serving others. By adopting a servant leadership mindset, new managers can build trust, foster collaboration, and empower their teams to achieve greater success. Embracing the principles of servant leadership can truly transform the way new managers lead and inspire others.

In addition to servant leadership, new managers should also be aware of situational, transactional, charismatic, bureaucratic, and adaptive leadership styles. Each of these approaches offers its own set of strategies and techniques for leading others. By exploring and understanding these various styles, new managers can expand their leadership toolkit and become more versatile and adaptable leaders.

Embracing the journey of leadership growth is essential for new managers as they navigate the complexities of leading others. By understanding and adopting different management styles, including servant leadership, new managers can enhance their effectiveness and impact as leaders. By continuously learning, growing, and evolving their leadership skills, new managers can become the kind of leaders who inspire, motivate, and empower others to achieve great things.

Making a Lasting Impact as a Servant Leader

In the world of management, there are various leadership styles that one can adopt in order to effectively lead a team. One such style that has gained popularity in recent years is servant leadership. This style focuses on serving others first, rather than being served, and has been proven to have a lasting impact on both individuals and organizations. For new managers looking to make a difference in their roles, adopting a servant leadership mindset can be the key to success.

One of the main principles of servant leadership is putting the needs of others before your own. This means taking the time to truly listen to your team members, understand their concerns, and provide them with the support and guidance they need to succeed. By showing empathy and compassion towards those you lead, you can build trust and create a positive work environment where everyone feels valued and appreciated.

Another important aspect of servant leadership is leading by example. As a new manager, it is crucial to demonstrate the values and behaviors that you expect from your team members. By being a role model and living out the principles of servant leadership in your daily interactions, you can inspire others to follow suit and create a culture of servanthood within your organization.

Servant leadership also involves empowering your team members to take ownership of their work and make decisions autonomously. By giving your employees the freedom to innovate and problem-solve on their own, you can foster a sense of ownership and accountability that will drive performance and productivity. This approach not only benefits the individual team members, but also the organization as a whole, leading to greater success and growth in the long run.

Making a lasting impact as a servant leader requires a commitment to serving others, leading by example, and empowering your team members to excel. By embracing the principles of servant leadership, new managers can create a positive work environment where everyone feels supported and valued. This leadership style not only benefits individuals on a personal level, but also contributes to the overall success and growth of the organization. As you embark on your journey in servant leadership, remember that the true measure of a leader is not in their title or position, but in the positive impact they have on those around them.

Conclusion: Your Journey to Leading with a Servant Heart

In conclusion, your journey to leading with a servant heart as a new manager is a challenging yet rewarding one. Throughout this book, we have explored various management styles and leadership approaches, including autocratic, democratic, laissez-faire, transformational, servant, situational, transactional, charismatic, bureaucratic, and adaptive leadership styles. Each of these styles has its own strengths and weaknesses, but it is clear that leading with a servant heart can bring about the most positive and sustainable results in the long run.

As a new manager, it is important to understand that servant leadership is not about being a pushover or letting others walk all over you. It is about putting the needs of your team members first, empowering them to reach their full potential, and creating a culture of trust, collaboration, and accountability. By leading with a servant heart, you can inspire your team to achieve great things and create a positive impact on your organization.

It is also crucial to remember that leading with a servant heart is a continuous journey of growth and self-improvement. As a new manager, you will face numerous challenges and obstacles along the way, but by staying true to your values and beliefs, you can overcome any obstacles that come your way. Remember to always seek feedback from your team members, be open to new ideas and perspectives, and be willing to adapt and evolve as a leader.

In the fast-paced and ever-changing world of business, it is essential for new managers to embrace servant leadership as a guiding philosophy. By focusing on serving others, building strong relationships, and fostering a culture of trust and collaboration, you can create a high-performing team that is motivated, engaged, and committed to achieving shared goals. Leading with a servant heart is not always easy, but it is definitely worth the effort in the long run.

In closing, I encourage you to continue on your journey to leading with a servant heart and to never lose sight of the impact you can make as a new manager. By embodying the values of servant leadership and striving to create a positive and empowering work environment for your team members, you can truly make a difference in the lives of others and leave a lasting legacy as a leader. Remember, leadership is not about titles or positions – it is about making a positive impact and inspiring others to be their best selves.